Teaching Little Fingers To Play Christmas Carols

Piano Solos with Optional Teacher Accompaniments

Arranged by
Carolyn Miller

CONTENTS

Cover Design by Nick Gressle

ISBN 978-0-87718-029-6

WILLIS MUSIC

EXCLUSIVELY DISTRIBUTED BY
HAL•LEONARD®
7777 W. BLUEMOUND RD. P.O. BOX 13819
MILWAUKEE, WISCONSIN 53213

Visit Hal Leonard Online at
www.halleonard.com

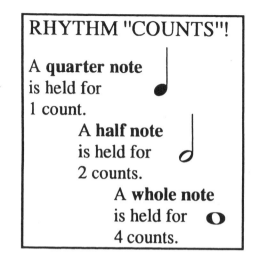

RHYTHM "COUNTS"!

A **quarter note**
is held for
1 count.

A **half note**
is held for
2 counts.

A **whole note**
is held for
4 counts.

Student Position
One Octave Higher When Performing as a Duet

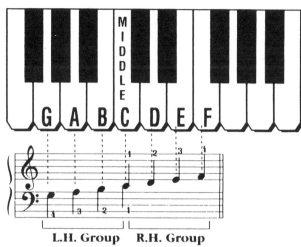

L.H. Group   R.H. Group

Jolly Old Saint Nicholas
Optional Teacher Accompaniment

Arr. Carolyn Miller

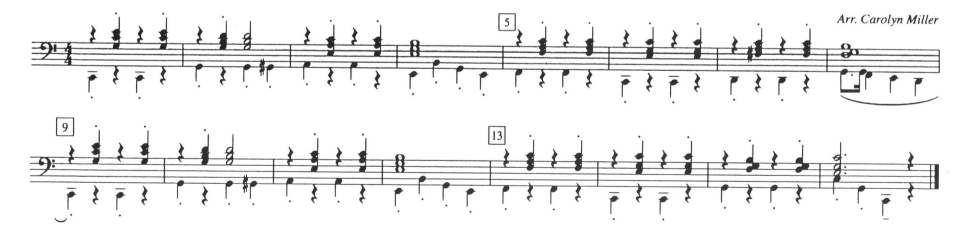

Jolly Old Saint Nicholas

Traditional
Arr. Carolyn Miller

Play both hands one octave higher when performing as a duet.

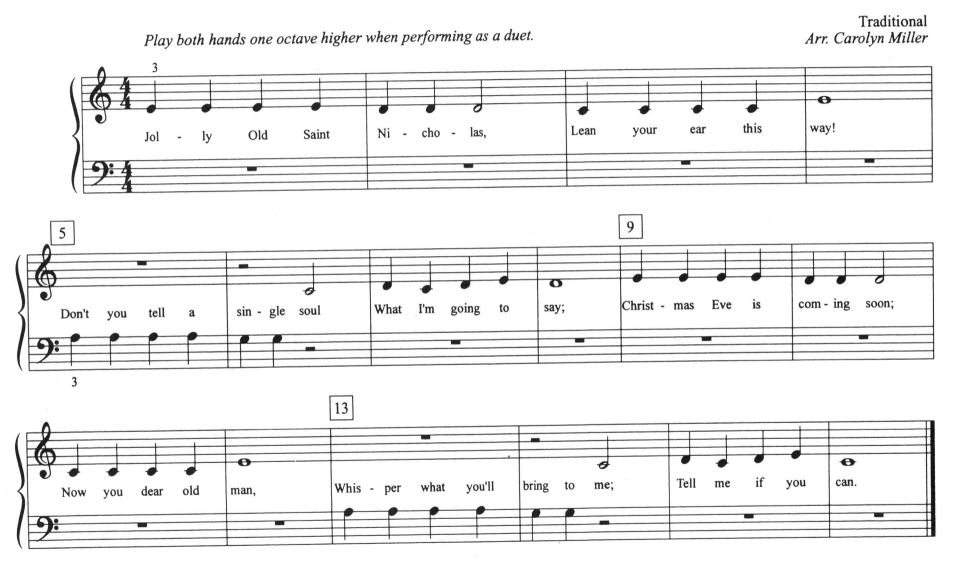

4

Student Position
One Octave Higher When Performing as a Duet

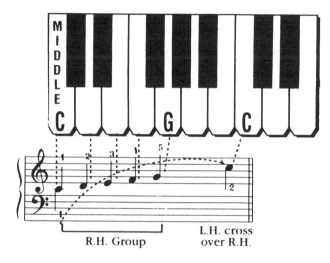

The time value of an eighth note ♪ is HALF as long as that of a quarter note. PlayTWO eighth notes to ONE count.

Jingle Bells
Optional Teacher Accompaniment

Arr. Carolyn Miller

Jingle Bells

Play both hands one octave higher when performing as a duet.

J. Pierpont
Arr. Carolyn Miller

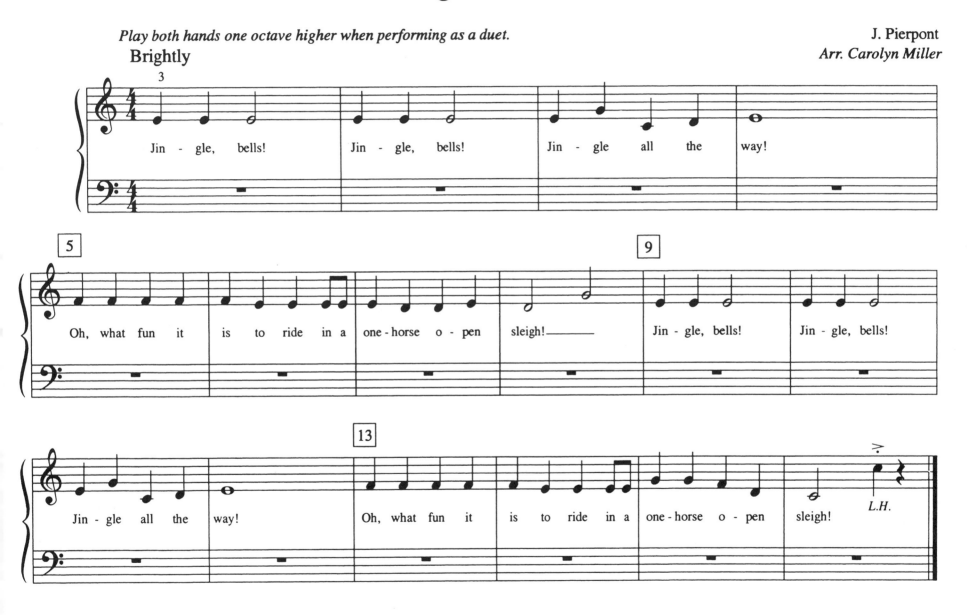

6

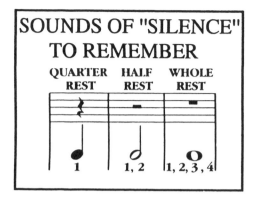

SOUNDS OF "SILENCE" TO REMEMBER

QUARTER REST	HALF REST	WHOLE REST
𝄽	▬	▬
♩	♪	𝅝
1	1, 2	1, 2, 3, 4

THE UPBEAT

This piece begins on a weak beat--the last count in a measure. You must therefore ACCENT the first beat after the bar line. The missing counts of the first measure will be found in the last measure of the piece.

O Come, All Ye Faithful

Optional Teacher Accompaniment

Arr. Carolyn Miller

O Come, All Ye Faithful

Latin Hymn, 17th Century
Tr. Canon Frederick Oakley

Old Latin
Arr. Carolyn Miller

ACCENTS
Always remember to **gently accent the first beat** of each measure when you are playing in 3/4 time!

LEFT or RIGHT?
When the stem of Middle C goes UP, play it with the *right hand*.
When the stem of Middle C goes DOWN, play it with the *left hand*!

We Three Kings of Orient Are
Optional Teacher Accompaniment

Arr. Carolyn Miller

with pedal

We Three Kings of Orient Are

Play both hands one octave higher when performing as a duet.

John Hopkins
Arr. Carolyn Miller

We three kings of O - ri - ent are; Bear - ing gifts we tra - verse a - far,

Field and foun - tain, moor and moun - tain, Fol - low - ing yon - der star. O——

Star of won - der, star of night, Star with roy - al beau - ty bright,

West - ward lead - ing, still pro - ceed - ing, Guide us to Thy per - fect light.

10

Up on the Housetop
Optional Teacher Accompaniment

Arr. Carolyn Miller

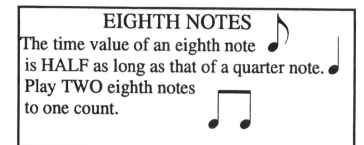

Up on the Housetop

Traditional
Arr. Carolyn Miller

Play both hands one octave higher when performing as a duet.

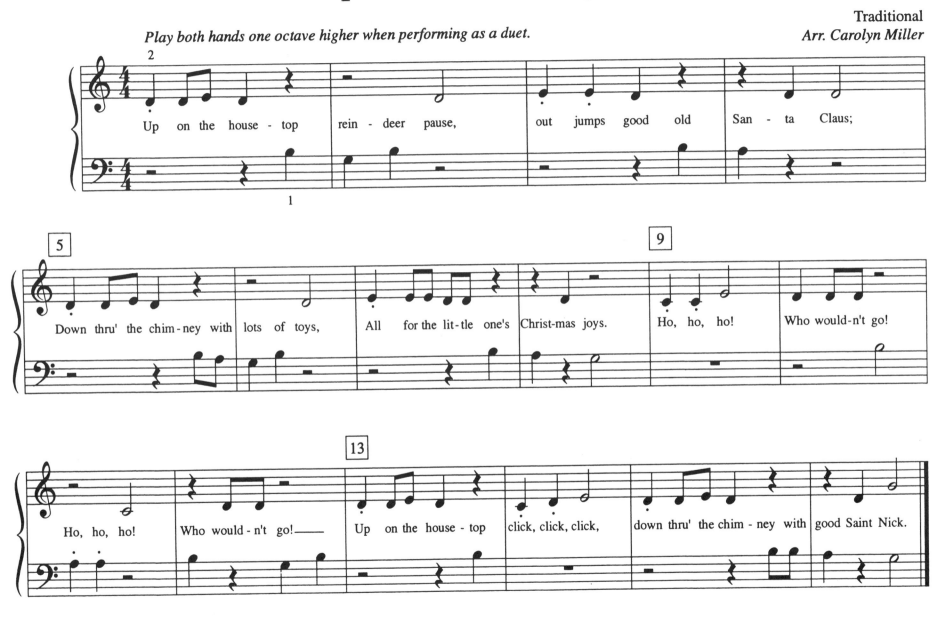

12

THE PHRASE
Groups of notes, like words in books, tell stories when they are arranged in "sentences" and punctuated. A curved line over a group of notes indicates MUSICAL SENTENCES called PHRASES.

LEFT OVER RIGHT!
Watch out for the **Treble Clef A** that the left hand gets to play! Take your left hand all the way over your right hand to play the A key above Middle C!

Hark! The Herald Angels Sing
Optional Teacher Accompaniment

Arr. Carolyn Miller

Hark! The Herald Angels Sing

Charles Wesley

Felix Mendelssohn
Arr. Carolyn Miller

Play one both hands octave higher when performing as a duet.

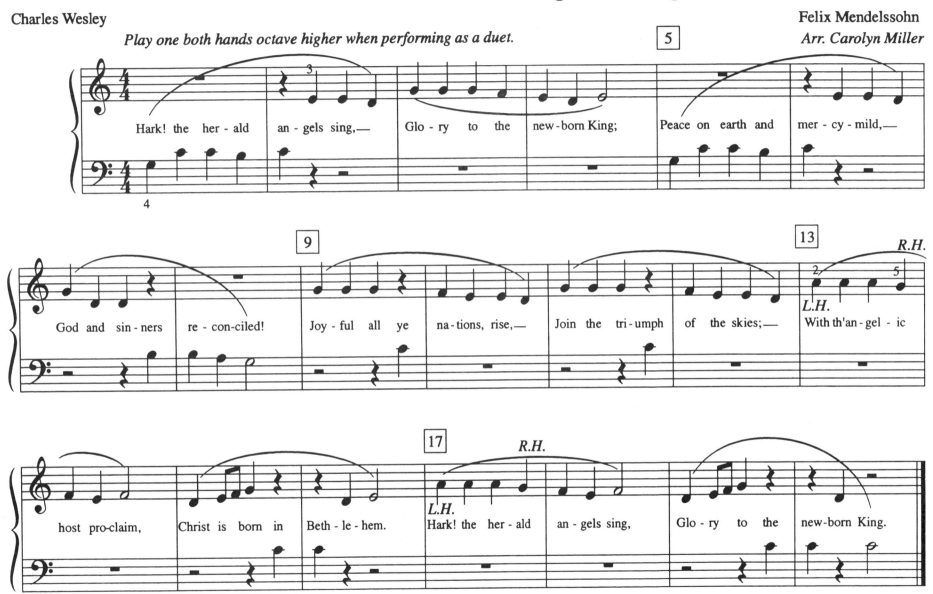

14

F SHARP

This is a sharp sign ♯. It means to play the first black key to the right of F.

THE TIE

The TIE is a curved line joining one note to another of the SAME PITCH, and means that the first note is to be held for the full value of both notes, without the second one being struck.

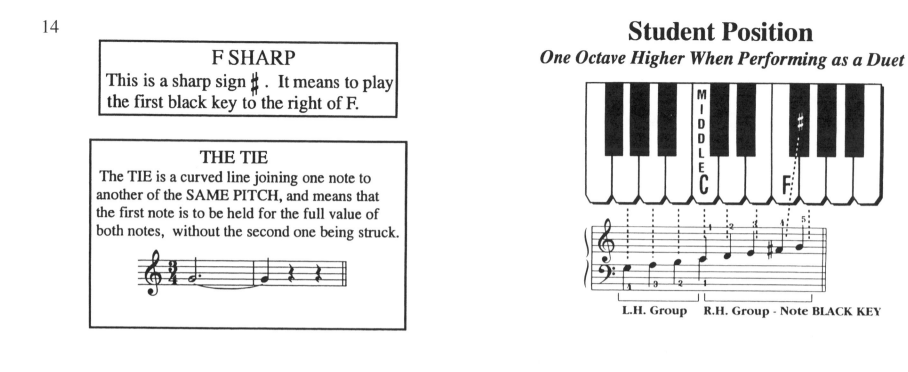

Student Position
One Octave Higher When Performing as a Duet

L.H. Group   R.H. Group - Note BLACK KEY

The First Noël
Optional Teacher Accompaniment

Arr. Carolyn Miller

The First Noël

Traditional

Play both hands one octave higher when performing as a duet.

18th Century French
Arr. Carolyn Miller

16

THE DOTTED HALF-NOTE
(THREE-BEAT NOTE)

HOLD 3 BEATS (1, 2, 3)
A DOT after a note increases
the value of that note by
one half.

PREPARATION
Locate, name and play
the L.H. Group and then
the R.H. Group.

Student Position

One Octave Higher When Performing as a Duet

L.H. Group   R.H. Group

Silent Night
Optional Teacher Accompaniment

Arr. Carolyn Miller

with pedal

Silent Night

Joseph Möhr

Franz Gruber
Arr. Carolyn Miller

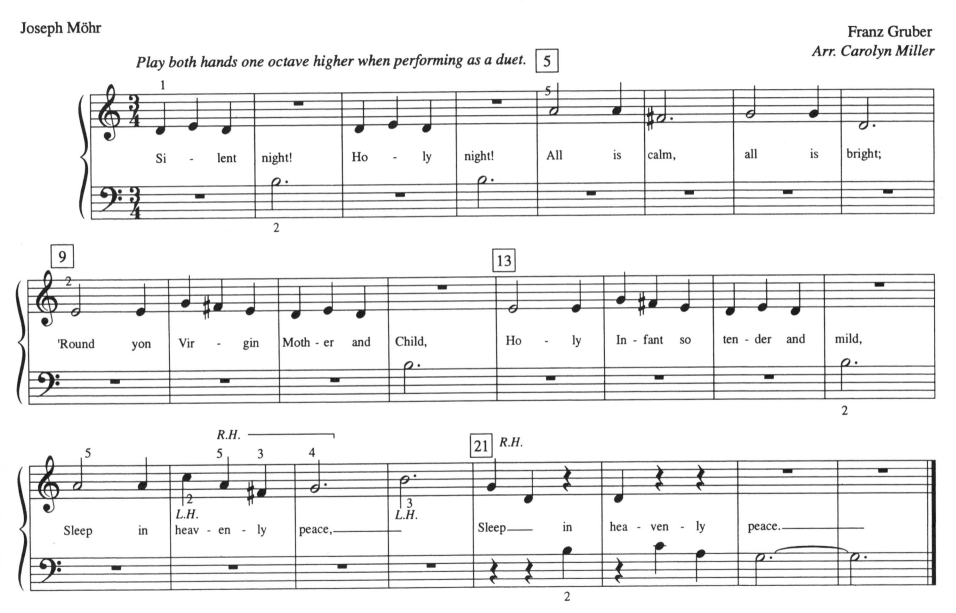

> ## Key Signature
> When the SHARP sign (♯) is placed between the clef sign and the time signature it becomes the KEY SIGNATURE. In this piece all F's must be sharped (played on the first black key to the right of F).

Joy to the World!
Optional Teacher Accompaniment

Arr. Carolyn Miller

Joy to the World!

Isaac Watts

George F. Handel
Arr. Carolyn Miller

Play both hands one octave higher when performing as a duet.

20

Review
This piece contains things you already know!
Don't forget your phrasing, eighth notes,
left hand over to A, tied notes, and F#'s!

Deck the Hall
Optional Teacher Accompaniment

Arr. Carolyn Miller

Deck the Hall

Traditional

Old Welsh
Arr. Carolyn Miller

Angels We Have Heard on High

Optional Teacher Accompaniment

Arr. Carolyn Miller

Angels We Have Heard on High

Traditional

French
Arr. Carolyn Miller

O Come, Little Children

C. von Schmidt

J.P.A. Schultz
Arr. Carolyn Miller

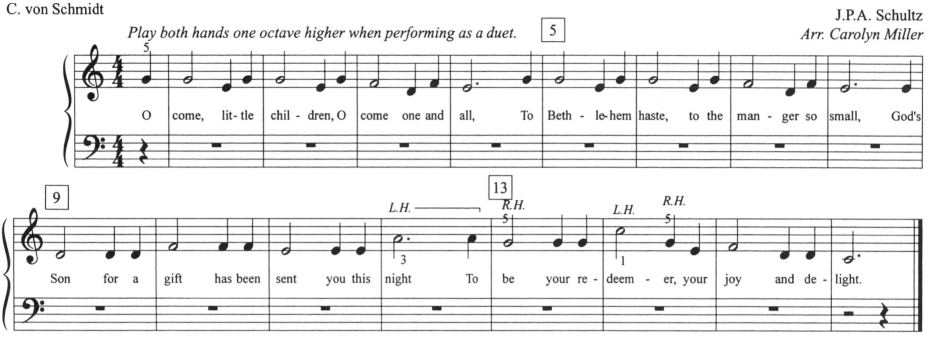

Play both hands one octave higher when performing as a duet.

O come, lit- tle chil - dren, O come one and all, To Beth - le-hem haste, to the man - ger so small, God's

Son for a gift has been sent you this night To be your re - deem - er, your joy and de - light.

Optional Teacher Accompaniment

Arr. Carolyn Miller